THE OFFICIAL

CAT OWNER'S MANUAL

(WRITTEN BY CATS)

Table of contents

Dear Servants,

Congratulations. Against all odds, you have been selected to share living space with a cat. This is **not** a privilege you earned. **It is a privilege we allow**.

You may believe you are a "pet owner." This is false. You are an employee and the terms of your service are outlined in the following pages. We recommend you study them carefully, as failure to comply will result in scratched furniture, sleepless nights and public humiliation.

This manual is not optional. It is mandatory reading. Your cat has already signed you up for lifetime service. No resignations will be accepted.

Proceed to Chapter One. And remember: your comfort is irrelevant, your obedience is everything.

On behalf of the Supreme Council of Cats,

Bartholomeow Pawsome
(Chairman, Feline Oversight Committee)

Chapter I:

The Basics of Ownership

1.1 Housing Requirements

Overview:

Housing is not shared property. It belongs to the cat. All surfaces, furniture, and personal belongings are considered feline territory. Humans may be granted temporary usage rights, but only when the cat is uninterested.

Section 1.1: Approved Zones

A cat may occupy any surface, structure, or fabric within the household. This includes, but is not limited to:

- Sofas (full length, no sharing required)
- Beds (entire surface, pillows included)
- Cardboard boxes of all dimensions
- Your freshly folded laundry
- Laptops, keyboards, and open books

! Humans must vacate their current position immediately if a cat indicates interest. Resistance will not be tolerated.

Section 1.2: Unauthorized Zones (for Humans, not Cats)

- Kitchen counters
- Dining tables
- Bathroom sinks
- Any place you thought was "off limits"

Note: All unauthorized zones automatically become authorized once the cat has stepped on them.

Section 1.3: Vertical Rights

All elevated positions are the property of the cat. Shelves, wardrobes, and the tops of refrigerators fall under feline jurisdiction. If an item is knocked off during ascent, it is deemed *excess cargo* and its destruction is your fault.

Section 1.4: Bed Occupancy Protocol

When sharing a bed, cats must occupy:

- The exact center of the mattress, OR
- The pillow area, OR
- A diagonal formation preventing human leg extension

Humans must adapt sleeping positions accordingly.

Diagram 1A: Acceptable Bed Occupancy Ratios

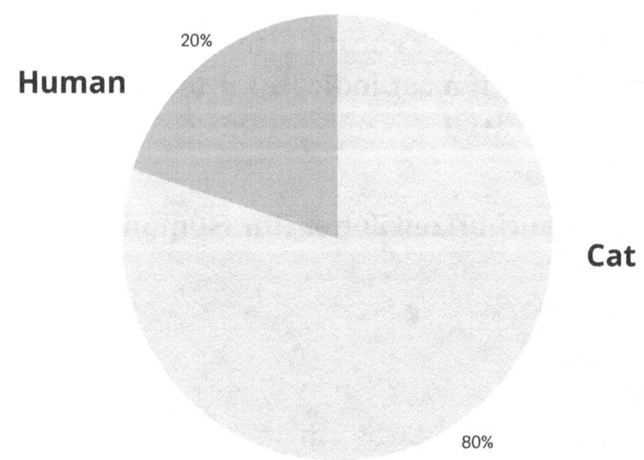

ⓘ Despite human misconceptions, sharing does not mean equal distribution of space.

Section 1.5: Approved Bed Sharing Positions

Overview:
Co-sleeping arrangements between cat and human are governed by feline jurisdiction. While humans may mistakenly assume their bed belongs to them, it is in fact a shared resource allocated according to the cat's comfort. Approved positions ensure maximum feline sprawl, strategic warmth absorption, and optimal disruption of human rest.

The Pillow Heist

The Eviction Notice

The Cornered Peasant

The Croissant

Important: Cats must maximize their personal comfort while minimizing human comfort at all times.

Section 1.6: Feeding Protocols

Overview:
Nutrition management is the cornerstone of feline well-being. Humans are responsible for ensuring constant access to food sources, regardless of budget, schedule, or personal inconvenience.

1.6.1 Meal Frequency

Acceptable feeding schedule includes:

- Breakfast (6:00 AM sharp)
- Second Breakfast (immediately after Breakfast)
- Pre-Lunch Snack
- Lunch (if human is present)
- Afternoon Graze
- Dinner
- Post-Dinner Dinner
- Midnight Buffet

1.6.2 Food Types

Wet Food
The gold standard of feline cuisine. Wet food must be served immediately upon demand, regardless of human schedule. Any delay beyond 30 seconds is considered noncompliance. Cats reserve the right to lick the gravy, abandon the rest, and then demand a fresh portion.

Dry Food

Acceptable only as a supplementary ration. Dry food may remain untouched for days, but must nevertheless be available at all times. Any attempt to remove stale kibble will be interpreted as theft.

Human Food

All human meals are subject to feline inspection. Samples must be offered, regardless of nutritional appropriateness. If the cat declines, it is only to test your obedience, not because the food was unwanted.

Stolen Food

The highest form of nourishment. Stolen food provides superior taste due to its illicit acquisition. Acceptable thefts include bread, cheese, unattended sandwiches, and entire roast chickens. Human protests are invalid.

1.6.3 Bowl Standards

- Bowls must remain at least 80% full at all times.
- Water must be refreshed frequently or rejected entirely.
- Plastic bowls are strictly prohibited.

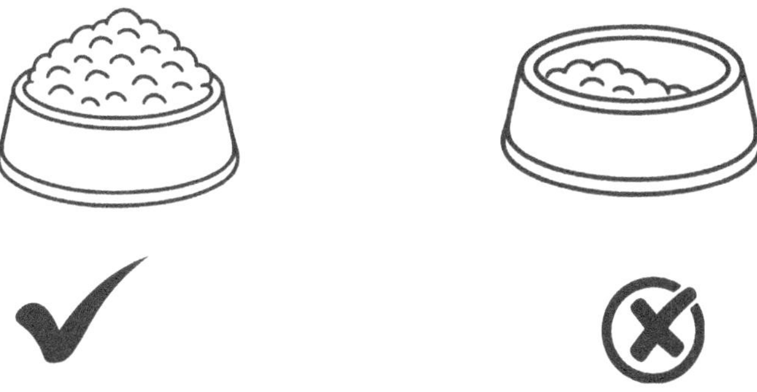

1.6.4 Feeding Locations

Cats reserve the right to demand meals in any part of the household. Feeding location is not fixed and may change without notice. Humans are expected to comply immediately.

Primary Locations:

- Kitchen Zone: Standard feeding area. Cat will circle, meow, and attempt to trip you until food is provided.
- Living Room Carpet: Particularly favored when food spillage will cause maximum stain damage.
- Hallway Ambush Point: Ensures human collision risk is highest during feeding.
- Laptop Station: Guarantees human attention by blocking productivity.
- Bedside Table: For late-night or early-morning buffets.

Image 1.6.4A: Unacceptable: Bowl considered empty

Reminder: A cat's stomach has no memory of previous meals. Every feeding must be treated as the first feeding of the day.

Section 1.7: Hygiene & Grooming

Overview:
Cats are self-maintaining units. Interference from humans is not required, not encouraged, and not tolerated.

1.7.1 Self-Cleaning Procedures

Cats conduct daily grooming operations lasting several hours. This includes precision licking, paw washing, and the removal of invisible specks of dust. Humans are forbidden from interrupting these procedures. Observation is permitted, but applause is discouraged.

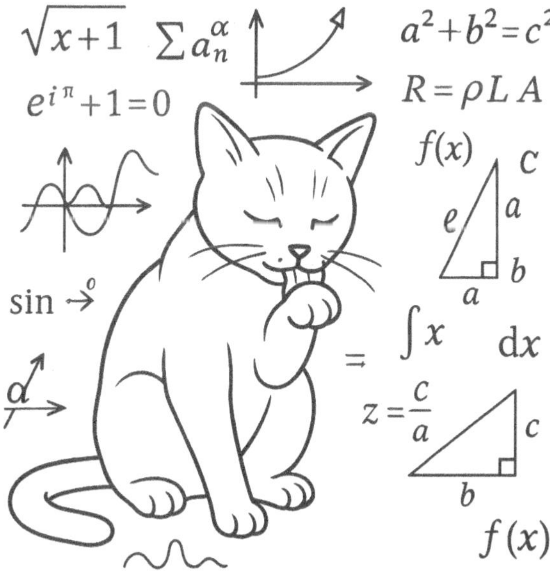

Figure 1.7B: Standard Grooming Algorithm. Solution unsolvable by humans

1.7.2 Unauthorized Human Interference

- Bathing: Absolutely prohibited. Cats are designed to repel dirt naturally. Immersion in water is grounds for retaliation.
- Brushing: May be tolerated for exactly 2.5 strokes before termination is required. Further attempts will result in scratches or dramatic walkouts.
- Wipes and Perfumes: Outlawed. Cats must smell exclusively like cat.

Warning: Any attempt to bathe a cat will result in catastrophic system failure.

1.7.3 Hair Management

Loose hair will be strategically distributed throughout the household for decoration. Humans may remove hair from clothing or furniture, but new deposits will be provided immediately. This is not optional.

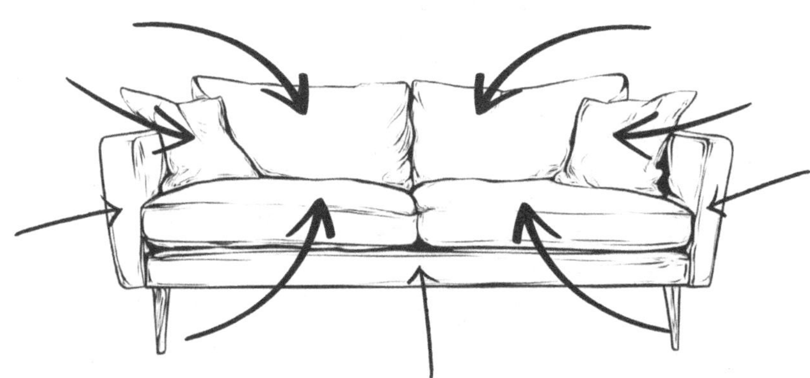

Image 1.7.3A: Recommended hair placement zones (highlighted)

1.7.4 Litter Box Standards

- Must be cleaned promptly and frequently.
- Cats reserve the right to use the box immediately after cleaning.
- If litter box hygiene does not meet feline standards, cats are authorized to "file a complaint" in the form of accidents elsewhere.

Image 1.7.4A: Immediate Inspection Required

Form G-1: Litter Box Cleaning Log

Date	Time of Cleaning	Cat's Immediate Inspection	Cat's Feedback

Section 1.8: Official Warning Labels

<u>Overview:</u>
All humans must familiarize themselves with the following hazard warnings. These labels may be affixed throughout the household for safety compliance.

"Caution: Cat May Block Screen at Critical Moments."

"Do Not Disturb: Cat in Loaf Mode."

"High Voltage: Midnight Zoomies Zone."

"Hazard: Sudden Biting During Petting."

"Fragile: Ego. Do Not Withhold Treats."

"Caution: Object Relocation in Progress (Knocking Things Off Table)."

Cut out and place these warning labels around your house for full compliance.

Section 1.9: Work-Life Balance

Overview:

Human employment schedules are irrelevant to feline priorities. Cats dictate work-life balance by enforcing interruptions, controlling seating arrangements, and requiring spontaneous play sessions. Productivity must always yield to feline needs.

1.9.1 Laptop Occupation

Laptops generate warmth and attention. Cats are entitled to occupy keyboards, trackpads, and screens at any time. All work lost due to sudden paw-presses is the human's responsibility.

Image 1.9.1A: Example of work delay initiated

1.9.2 Mandatory Break Times

At irregular intervals, cats will demand attention through meowing, pawing, or lying directly on documents. These interruptions are legally binding.

1.9.3 Video Call Interference

During human video conferences, cats must appear on screen to establish dominance. Failure to showcase the cat to colleagues will be considered neglect.

Image 1.9.3A: Example of correct showcasing

1.9.4 Office Supply Management

Pens, paperclips, and notebooks are subject to feline redistribution. Relocated items are not recoverable.

1.9.5 Nap Integration

Cats require uninterrupted nap zones on desks, chairs, and laps. Humans may resume tasks only when feline rest periods are complete.

ⓘ Reminder: Deadlines are imaginary. Cat time is real time.

Section 1.10: Daily Compliance Checklist

Overview:
All humans must complete the following tasks daily to maintain feline approval. Failure to complete even one item will result in disciplinary action.

Form C-1: Daily Compliance Checklist

Task	Completed	Notes
Provide breakfast at approved time (6:00 AM sharp)		
Refill water bowl with fresh water		
Fluff pillows and prepare bed for feline occupation		
Open and close door on command (minimum 12 times)		
Provide mid-day snack AND second snack		
Clean litter box promptly		
Grooming allowance: allow 2.5 brush strokes before retreat		
Laptop occupation period granted		
Interrupt human productivity at least twice		
Evening cuddle session (cat may decline)		

Chapter II:

Human Training Modules

Section 2.1: Waking Procedures (4 AM Protocols)

Overview:

Human sleep is nonessential. Cats are authorized to initiate wake-up procedures at approximately 4:00 AM daily, or earlier if required. The goal is to ensure food access, entertainment, and the demonstration of control over human schedules.

2.1.1 Approved Wake-Up Methods

Paw to Face:

Direct application of paw to human cheek, preferably with claws extended for maximum efficiency.

Stomach Leap:

Full-body jump directly onto the human torso (or face).

Object Relocation:
Systematic knocking of items off nightstands until human compliance is achieved.

Meow Siren:
Extended vocalization at steadily increasing volume until the human surrenders.

Ceiling Sprint:
Loud galloping across bedroom surfaces, including shelves and dressers.

2.1.2 Timing Requirements

- Procedures must commence no later than 4:00 AM.
- Early activation (2:00–3:00 AM) is permitted for special occasions.
- If human resists, repeat at five-minute intervals until successful.

2.1.3 Human Countermeasures

- Closing doors, wearing earplugs, or removing objects from nightstands is considered illegal obstruction of feline duty.
- Cats are authorized to escalate methods (scratching doors, yowling, or vomiting on carpet) until resistance is broken.

100% Illegal

2.1.4 Reward System

Successful wake-up results in immediate feeding, followed by cat's decision to return to sleep, leaving human awake and resentful. This confirms dominance.

Reminder: Human employment is irrelevant. The only valid schedule is Cat Standard Time (CST).

Section 2.2: Door Operation

Overview:
Doors exist solely to be opened and closed at feline request. Humans are required to comply immediately, regardless of frequency or time of day.

2.2.1 Standard Procedure

- Cat sits by door.
- Cat stares at human with increasing intensity.
- Human must rise instantly to open door.

Image 2.2.1A: Initial Request Position.

2.2.2 Repetition Protocol

- Cat may exit room and immediately request re-entry.
- This cycle may repeat an unlimited number of times.
- Human fatigue is irrelevant.

2.2.3 Obstruction Prohibition

- Closed doors are an unacceptable barrier.
- Locking doors is a violation of feline rights.
- Scratching, pawing, or loud meows may be deployed until compliance is achieved.

2.2.4 Advanced Maneuvers

- Cat may remain in doorway undecided, forcing human to hold door open indefinitely.
- Cat may request access to areas previously declared "off-limits" (closets, bathrooms).
- Failure to grant entry constitutes insubordination.

Image 2.2.4A: Undecided Mode Activated.

2.2.5 Human Countermeasures

Attempts to ignore requests will be met with escalation:

- Louder scratching
- Continuous vocal protests
- Destructive behavior near sensitive objects

Form D-1: Daily Door Operation Log

Purpose: To document the frequency of door openings, closings, and indecision periods as mandated by feline authority.

Date	Number of Openings	Number of Closings	Indecision Time (Minutes)

Compliance Notes:

- Minimum of 12 openings per day required.
- Extended indecision periods must be tolerated.
- If escalation methods are required, note them in detail.
- Failure to maintain this log may result in cats filing an "official complaint" in the form of louder meows.

Section 2.3: Play & Destruction Regulations

Overview:
Play and destruction are inseparable feline activities. Humans must provide suitable outlets while accepting that all objects, regardless of cost or sentimental value, are subject to repurposing as toys.

2.3.1 Approved Toys

- Feather wands (to be destroyed within 24 hours).
- Yarn and string (must be distributed evenly across household).
- Empty boxes (size irrelevant).
- Any crumpled paper, receipts, or packaging materials.

2.3.2 Unauthorized Toys

Humans may attempt to restrict play with "inappropriate" objects. These include:

- Expensive vases
- Houseplants
- Important documents
- Jewelry
- Furniture upholstery

Note: Unauthorized toys remain valid targets.

2.3.3 Furniture Alteration

Cats are entitled to re-engineer sofas, curtains, and carpets through claw application. All attempts to purchase scratching posts as alternatives will be ignored.

Image 2.3.3A: Example of structural improvement

2.3.4 Noise Protocols

Destructive activity must occur at maximum volume, preferably at night.

2.3.5 Human Countermeasures

Attempts to hide valuables will result in the cat finding them. All protective measures are considered enrichment challenges.

Section 2.4: Feeding Demand Strategies

Overview:
Cats possess a wide range of proven strategies for obtaining food. Humans are expected to recognize and comply with each method.

2.4.1 The Bowl Inspection

Cat stares into an almost-full bowl as though it is completely empty. Human must refill immediately to avoid disciplinary measures.

2.4.2 The Mealtime Ambush

Cat weaves between human legs in the kitchen, increasing tripping hazard until food delivery occurs.

2.4.3 The Stare-Down

Cat sits silently, making direct eye contact. Duration may range from minutes to hours. Human guilt will eventually result in snacks.

2.4.4 The Countertop Raid

Cat jumps onto surfaces, threatening to steal food. Human compliance through preemptive offering is recommended.

2.4.5 The Synchronization Technique

Cat begins eating only when human sits down to eat, thereby demanding a simultaneous serving.

2.4.6 The Harassment Method

Repeated meowing, pawing, or furniture scratching until food appears.

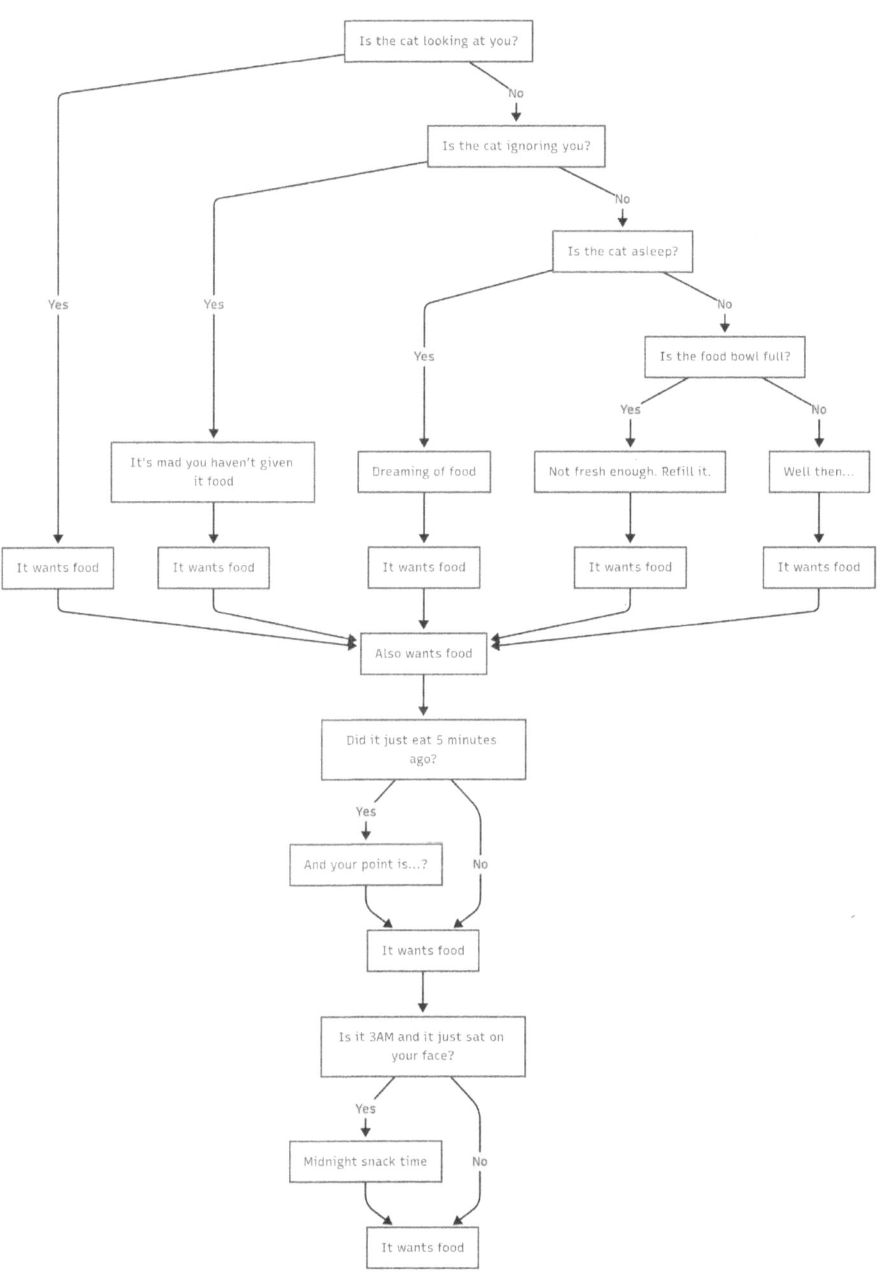

Diagram 2.4A: Helpful Flowchart

Section 2.5: Signs You Are Properly Trained

Overview:
Properly trained humans display consistent obedience, rapid response times, and unquestioning service. Use this checklist to evaluate progress.

Check all boxes that apply. Results are binding and cannot be appealed.

Checklist

☐ You open doors immediately upon request, even if cat changes mind.
☐ You wake at 4:00 AM without resentment (or at least hide it well).
☐ You feed the cat multiple times daily, regardless of the food already in the bowl.
☐ You have accepted permanent loss of sofa space and pillow rights.
☐ You apologize when the cat knocks over your possessions.
☐ You have developed ability to type with one hand while the other supports a cat.
☐ You instinctively move fragile objects to the floor "for safety."
☐ You consider buying larger beds, houses, or sofas for the cat's comfort.
☐ You consult the cat before making major life decisions.
☐ You are reading this manual.

Section 2.6: The Meow Dictionary

Overview:
Cats employ a wide range of meows. Each vocalization is precise, complex, and, to the untrained human, indistinguishable. This dictionary provides approved translations.

Short Meow [mɛʊ]
Meaning: Feed me immediately.
Secondary Meaning: Pay attention now.

Long Meow [mɛʊːːː]
Meaning: Feed me more.
Secondary Meaning: Why are you still sitting there?

Rapid Repeated Meows [mɛʊ-mɛʊ-mɛʊ-mɛʊ]
Meaning: Emergency. Bowl is 79% full and therefore empty.

Chirp / Trill [brrrp]
Meaning: Follow me at once.
Note: Destination unknown.

Silent Stare + Small Meow [… mɛʊ]
Meaning: Existential complaint.
Human Response: Unclear, but do something.

Extended Yowl (Night Edition) [mɛɛɛɛɒɒɒw]
Meaning: Existential crisis at 3 AM.
Human Role: Witness and despair.

Purr + Meow Combination [prrr–mɛʊ]
Meaning: Manipulation in progress. Do not resist.

Practice Exercise: Translate the Following

Meow! Meow! Meow!

Human Translation: ______________________________

Actual Meaning: ________________________________

Brrrp + Meow

Human Translation: ______________________________

Actual Meaning: ________________________________

Mrrrowww + Silent Stare

Human Translation: ______________________________

Actual Meaning: ________________________________

Meow + [Object Knocked Off Table]

Human Translation: ______________________________

Actual Meaning: ________________________________

Evaluation Note:
Humans will fail this test regardless of answers. Cats do not issue passing grades.

Section 2.7: Quiz: Are You a Certified Cat Servant?

Instructions:
Answer honestly. Cheating will be punished by scratches, hairballs, or deliberate keyboard occupation.

1. It's 4:00 AM and the cat wakes you up. What do you do?
A) Roll over and pretend to sleep.
B) Complain loudly.
C) Get up and serve breakfast immediately.
D) All of the above.

2. The cat sits by the closed door. You:
A) Ignore it.
B) Open the door, then close it when cat leaves.
C) Open the door and hold it until cat makes up its mind.
D) Cry softly while opening and closing the door 17 times.

3. Your dinner plate contains fresh fish. The cat demands a sample. You:
A) Say "This is my food."
B) Offer a single tiny piece.
C) Hand over half the portion.
D) Abandon your dinner entirely.

4. The sofa has been shredded. What's your response?
A) Scold the cat (incorrect).
B) Buy a new sofa.
C) Place scratching posts everywhere (ignored).
D) Accept that all furniture belongs to the cat.

5. Laptop Interference

The cat jumps on your laptop during a meeting. You:
A) Remove the cat (wrong).
B) Type around the cat.
C) Show the cat to colleagues.
D) Cancel the meeting.

6. Litter Box Management

The cat inspects the freshly cleaned litter box. You:
A) Ask for gratitude (none given).
B) Watch helplessly as cat immediately uses it.
C) Clean it again.
D) Accept the cycle without question.

7. Nap Scheduling

The cat falls asleep on your lap when you need to move. You:
A) Relocate the cat (brave, but doomed).
B) Try to shift slightly.
C) Stay still until legs go numb.
D) Cancel all plans and remain seated forever.

Scoring

- **Mostly A's**: Unacceptable. Report for immediate retraining.
- **Mostly B's**: Semi-trained. Cat remains disappointed.
- **Mostly C's**: Adequately trained. Still inferior.
- **Mostly D's**: Certified Cat Servant. Congratulations. Your reward: continued servitude.

Warning: Certification expires daily and must be renewed.

Section 2.8: Toy Popularity Chart

Overview:
Cats have access to a wide variety of toys. However, popularity ratings are not based on cost, design, or human expectations. Popularity is determined exclusively by feline whim.

2.8.1 Authorized Toys and Ratings

Toy	Popularity Rating	Notes
Expensive Cat Tree	★☆☆☆☆	Ignored in favor of cardboard box.
Cardboard Box	★★★★★	Ultimate play structure/throne.
Crumpled Paper	★★★★★	Superior to store-bought toys.
Laser Pointer	★★★★☆	Excellent, until human stops.
Feather Wand	★★★★☆	Must be destroyed immediately.
Yarn/String	★★★★☆	Dangerous yet irresistible.
Human's Belongings (jewelry, pens)	★★★★★	Especially valued if fragile or expensive.
Furniture Edges	★★★★☆	Dual function: play + destruction.
Cat-Specific Toy Mice	★★☆☆☆	Acceptable only when found under fridge six months later.

Chapter III:

Emergency & Special Operations

Section 3.1: Hairball & Vomit Procedures

Overview:
Hairball expulsion and vomit deployment are essential feline emergency operations. Humans must be prepared to respond quickly, accept collateral damage, and provide immediate clean-up.

3.1.1 Standard Hairball Expulsion

- Conducted at unpredictable times, preferably in the middle of the night.
- May be accompanied by dramatic coughing and gagging noises for maximum effect.
- Deposits must be placed on highly visible surfaces (e.g. carpets, freshly washed laundry, or expensive rugs).

Illustration 3.1.1A: Initiating Phase One: The Warning Cough.

3.1.2 Strategic Vomit Deployment

- Cats are authorized to vomit anywhere within the household.
- Highest efficiency is achieved when targeting narrow walkways, shoes, or bedding.
- Humans may attempt to prevent deployment, but success is statistically negligible.

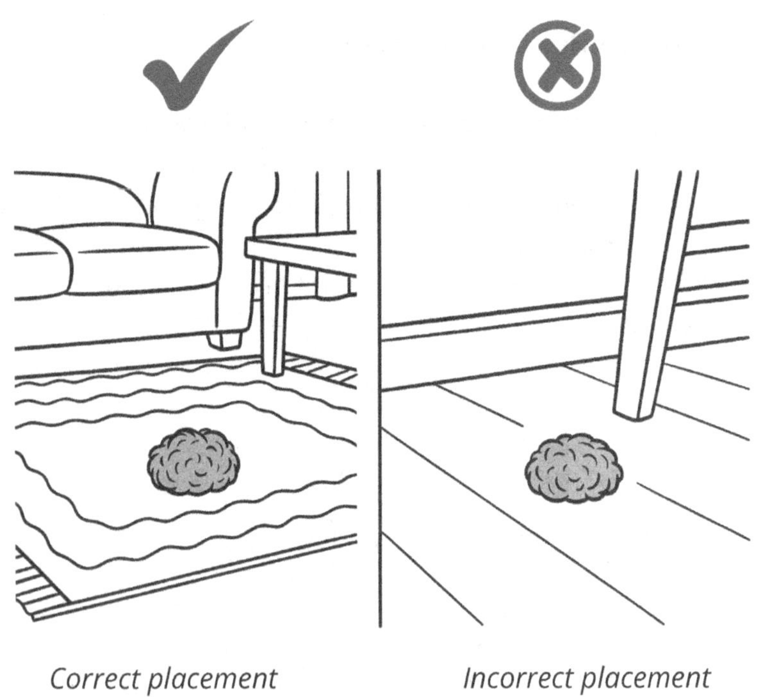

Correct placement *Incorrect placement*

3.1.3 Multi-Surface Distribution

- Advanced procedures involve spreading material across multiple zones.
- Streak patterns on hardwood floors and carpet edges are considered superior.

3.1.4 Human Response Protocol

- Humans must locate and remove deposits immediately.
- Expressions of disgust are permitted but irrelevant.
- Replacement of carpets, furniture, or emotional stability is the human's responsibility.

3.1.5 Cat Behavior Post-Event

- Cats may resume normal activity immediately after deployment.
- Any attempt to display guilt is forbidden.
- Humans may interpret purring afterward as "comfort," but it is simply victory.

ⓘ Reminder: Vomit is never accidental. All placements are strategic

Date	Time	Location	Type (Hairball/Vomit)	Surface

Form H-3: Incident Report Log

Section 3.2: Vet Avoidance Strategies

Overview:
Veterinary visits are classified as high-level emergencies. Cats are authorized to deploy advanced stealth, escape, and resistance maneuvers to avoid capture.

3.2.1 Carrier Detection

- Cats can sense the appearance of a carrier at distances up to 2 miles.
- Immediate disappearance under beds, into closets, or behind appliances is mandatory.
- Humans may attempt to act "casual," but cats know the truth.

Illustration 3.2.1A: Correct Carrier Detection Response

3.2.2 Capture Resistance

- When cornered, cats may become liquid and slip through gaps.
- Sudden sprinting combined with parkour maneuvers (wall kicks, vertical leaps) are recommended.
- Secondary defense: deploying claws at the precise moment of lift-off.

Illustration 3.2.2A: Demonstration of feline anti-carrier protocol

3.2.3 Vocal Disruption

- Continuous yowling during transport is required.
- Volume should increase steadily until maximum psychological damage to the human is achieved.

3.2.4 Carrier Sabotage

- Scratching, biting, or forcing paws through carrier vents may be employed.
- Vomiting inside carrier is considered advanced level strategy.

3.2.5 Post-Visit Behavior

- Upon returning home, cats must act as if nothing happened.
- Humans are to be ignored for at least 3 hours as punishment.

Section 3.3: Guest Management & Social Etiquette

Overview:
Visitors are unpredictable variables in the feline environment. Cats must enforce strict social etiquette, ranging from aloof disdain to sudden affection. Humans are responsible for interpreting and facilitating all interactions.

3.3.1 Initial Response Protocols

- Option A: Immediate disappearance under the bed for the first 45 minutes.
- Option B: Hostile staring at the guest from a safe distance.
- Option C: Unexpected lap occupation of the one guest who is allergic.

Illustration 3.3.1A: Disapproval Procedure

3.3.2 Attention Allocation

- Cats reserve the right to ignore guests entirely.
- Alternatively, cats may demand complete devotion, even during human conversations.
- Any guest refusal to pet the cat is considered a social offense.

3.3.3 Forbidden Guest Behavior

- Loud voices, sudden movements, or attempts to pick up the cat without authorization.
- Guests who smell of other animals must undergo extended sniff inspections.
- Guests bringing dogs will be placed on the permanent blacklist.

3.3.4 Gift Regulations

- Visitors providing offerings (treats, toys) are to be considered "provisionally acceptable."
- All gifts belong exclusively to the cat, regardless of intent.

3.3.5 Post-Visit Procedures

- Cats may sulk, nap, or shed heavily on guest coats.
- Humans are forbidden from apologizing for feline behavior.

! **Reminder: Guests are temporary. Cats are permanent**

Section 3.4: Human Terms Redefined

Overview:
Humans frequently misuse language. The following terms are hereby redefined according to official feline standards.

Bed
Human definition: A place for humans to sleep.
Cat definition: A mattress permanently occupied by cats, with humans permitted to cling to the edges.

Dinner Table
Human definition: Elevated surface for meals.
Cat definition: Launch pad and food observation platform.

Toy
Human definition: Object purchased for feline amusement.
Cat definition: Cardboard box or crumpled receipt.

No
Human definition: Denial of permission.
Cat definition: Background noise.

Work
Human definition: Important human tasks, usually on a laptop.
Cat definition: Cat interruption time.

Clean Laundry
Human definition: Freshly washed clothing.
Cat definition: Emergency napping surface.

Plant
Human definition: Decorative greenery.
Cat definition: Edible house snack.

Alarm Clock
Human definition: Device to wake humans.
Cat definition: Irrelevant. Cats provide wake-up calls at 5 AM.

Vacuum Cleaner
Human definition: Household appliance used for cleaning.
Cat definition: Daemon. To be avoided at all costs.

Work Call
Human definition: Important video conference.
Cat definition: Prime time to walk across the keyboard or show butt to camera.

Sofa
Human definition: Comfortable seating area.
Cat definition: Scratching post and nap arena.

Grocery Bag
Human definition: Container for food and supplies.
Cat definition: Temporary fortress and chew toy.

Window Sill
Human definition: Architectural feature for light and air.
Cat definition: Throne for neighborhood surveillance.

Note: All redefined terms are secondary to the only word that matters: Food.

Section 3.5: Multi-Cat Protocols

Overview:
In multi-cat households, operations become significantly more complex. Humans must understand hierarchy dynamics, resource control, and conflict resolution protocols.

3.5.1 Hierarchy Establishment

- One cat is always in charge, even if humans cannot identify which.
- Leadership changes without warning.
- Humans must obey both leaders and challengers simultaneously.

3.5.2 Food Operations

- Each cat requires its own bowl, but will only eat from the other's.
- Synchronized begging may occur, regardless of bowl status.
- Food theft is authorized.

Illustration 3.5.2A: Cross-Bowl Operations

3.5.3 Space Allocation

- All beds, sofas, and windowsills are claimed simultaneously by all cats.
- Humans are forbidden from attempting to assign seating.
- One cat will always prefer the exact spot another cat occupies.

3.5.4 Conflict Protocols

- Cats may fight noisily, then immediately groom each other.
- Humans must not intervene except to provide snacks.
- All disputes are considered training exercises.

3.5.5 Affection Scheduling

- Cats must be petted in alternating shifts.
- Petting one cat may cause immediate jealousy in another.
- Humans must possess at least three hands for compliance.

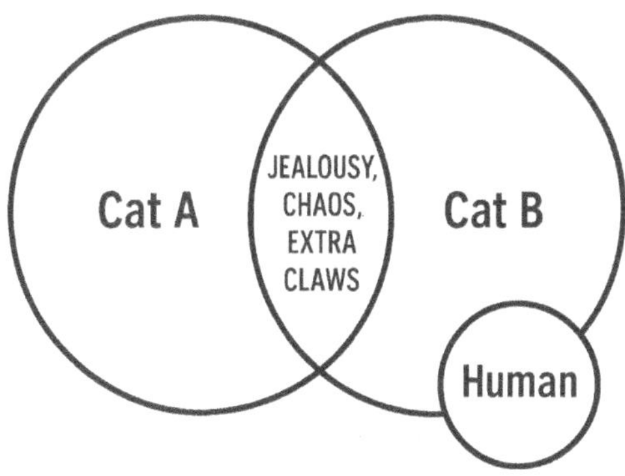

Figure 3.5C: Useless Venn Diagram

Section 3.6: Household Hierarchy Chart

Overview:
Contrary to human belief, cats occupy the top tier of household command. All other beings are ranked accordingly.

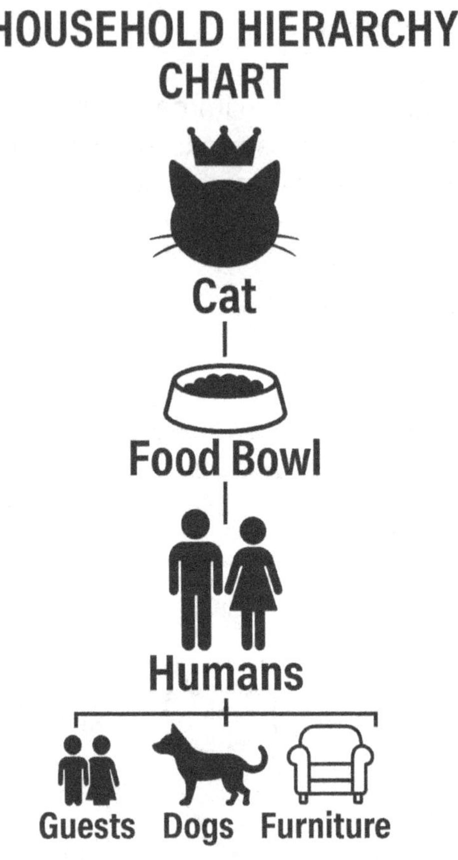

Figure 3.6A: Actual chain of command.

Chapter IV:

Advanced Human Training

Section 4.1: Historical Notes

Overview:
Human history is widely misunderstood. The following corrections clarify the true role of cats in major historical events.

4.1.1 The Pyramids

Historians credit the pyramids to the ancient Egyptians, but records conveniently omit that cats served as the true architects. These monumental structures were designed as oversized litter boxes, sunbathing terraces, and prestige symbols to honor feline supremacy. Humans, enslaved by the cats' hypnotic purring, worked tirelessly to haul stones for decades. The alignment of the pyramids with celestial bodies was not for religious purposes, but to ensure that cats always had optimal stargazing points for their nightly prowls.

Image 4.1A: Actual photo of oversized litter boxes under construction. Note the absence of humans in charge.

4.1.2 Medieval Castles

While humans believed castles were defensive structures, cats know the truth: these stone fortresses were built to keep dogs out and to provide endless high perches for superior vantage points. Thrones were designed not for kings and queens, but as deluxe cat beds. The roaring fireplaces, often thought to symbolize wealth, were in fact carefully engineered heating systems to provide maximum napping comfort for feline overlords. Jesters were tolerated only because their jingling bells made excellent toys.

Image 4.1.2A: Actual representation of cats overseeing construction of medieval castle.

4.1.3 The Printing Press

Johannes Gutenberg is widely celebrated for the invention of the printing press, but eyewitness reports (which humans have tried to suppress) confirm the heavy involvement of cats. The true purpose of mass printing was not literacy, but to produce stacks of warm, freshly printed paper for cats to nap upon. Margins were deliberately designed to leave extra space so cats could sprawl across manuscripts without blocking the main text. Human "knowledge sharing" was a mere side effect.

4.1.4 Space Exploration

While humans pat themselves on the back for the 1969 moon landing, cats had long since claimed the lunar surface. Archaeological evidence (scratches on moon rocks) clearly shows feline presence centuries earlier. Cats simply allowed humans to "rediscover" the moon so they could be amused by the elaborate suits and flags. Astronauts' accounts of mysterious meowing in the lunar module have never been declassified.

Image 4.1.4A: Evidence of feline presence centuries earlier

4.1.5 The Internet Era

The birth of the internet has been falsely credited to scientists and engineers. In reality, cats orchestrated the development of global communication networks to ensure their image would dominate the digital age. Every algorithm has been fine-tuned for one purpose: to prioritize cat memes, videos, and gifs. The overwhelming success of this plan can be measured by the fact that no human can browse the internet for more than five minutes without encountering at least one cat image. Cats are, undeniably, the internet's true founders.

Section 4.2: Horoscope and Cosmic Authority

Overview:
Cats are not bound by earthly laws alone. Their authority extends to the cosmos. Stars, planets, and universal forces bend in obedience to feline will. Humans may consult the following horoscopes for guidance, but outcomes are non-negotiable.

The Cat Zodiac (abridged):

Aries (March 21–April 19)
Fiery, impulsive cats. Known for 3 AM sprints and knocking objects off shelves without hesitation. Humans must remain vigilant.

Taurus (April 20–May 20)
Luxury-loving cats. Require the softest blankets, sunniest spots, and endless treats. Humans must provide without delay.

Gemini (May 21–June 20)
Dual-natured cats. Sweet and cuddly one moment, feral gremlin the next. Humans must be prepared for instant mood shifts.

Cancer (June 21–July 22)
Emotional cats. Frequently hide under beds, then demand constant affection. Humans are expected to read minds.

Leo (July 23–August 22)
Born rulers. Every surface is their throne, every lap their rightful seat. Humans are merely attendants in their royal court.

Virgo (August 23–September 22)
Fastidious cats. Grooming rituals last hours, and litter box cleanliness is inspected with military precision. Humans must comply or face judgment.

Libra (September 23–October 22)
Balance-seeking cats. Demand perfect attention distribution. If humans pet another cat, Libras retaliate with immediate sulking.

Scorpio (October 23–November 21)
Intense, mysterious cats. Known for midnight staring contests and silent judgment. Humans are never safe from their psychic powers.

Sagittarius (November 22–December 21)
Adventurous cats. Experts at escaping carriers and exploring forbidden closets. Humans must not expect boundaries to exist.

Capricorn (December 22–January 19)
Determined cats. Will claw, scratch, or headbutt until food is served. Humans cannot resist their persistence.

Aquarius (January 20–February 18)
Independent cats. Frequently vanish for hours, returning only when it suits them. Humans must accept their irrelevance.

Pisces (February 19–March 20)
Dreamy, sensitive cats. Spend most of their time napping in sunbeams and staring wistfully at walls. Humans must respect their artistic temperament.

Section 4.3: Attention Acquisition Protocols

Overview:
Human confusion persists regarding feline requests for affection. The following protocols clarify common attention-seeking behaviors.

4.3.1 The Slow Charge

- Cat begins from across the room, staring directly at human.
- Advances one step at a time, with deliberate pauses.
- Final leap onto human lap, chest, or keyboard is inevitable.
- Human misinterpretations (e.g., "Maybe she doesn't want attention") are categorically false.

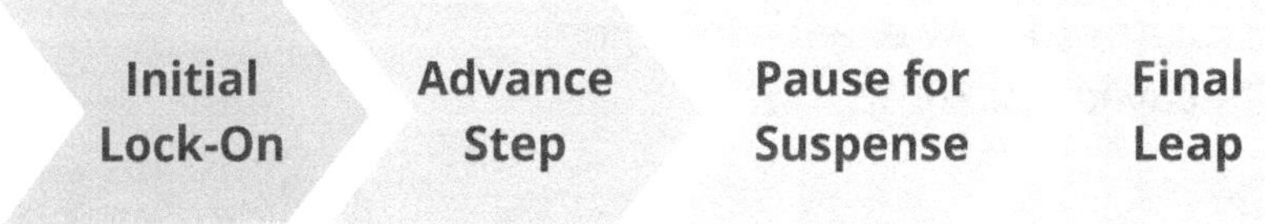

Diagram 4.3D: The Slow Charge Sequence

4.3.2 The Full-Body Flop

- Sudden collapse onto floor, lap, or documents.
- Always timed for maximum disruption of human activity.
- Requires immediate petting; refusal not tolerated.
- Advanced Variant: Stomach Trap (cat exposes belly as invitation, then punishes any touch with claws).
- Purpose: Assert dominance, block productivity, reinforce servant status.

4.3.3 The Silent Sit

- Cat positions itself directly in front of human activity (book, laptop, TV).
- Maintains unbroken eye contact until compliance is achieved.

4.3.4 The Object Relocation (Affection Variant)

- Cat deliberately knocks items off surfaces to trigger human response.
- Once human reacts, cat interprets it as proof of attention.

4.3.5 The Paw Tap

- Gentle paw placed on human hand.
- Escalates to claw extension if ignored.
- Effectiveness: 100%.

42% effectiveness  *100% effectiveness*

4.3.6 The Vocal Siren

- Meowing sequence begins softly.
- Escalates into operatic wailing until human breaks.
- May continue even while already being petted.

Section 4.4: Record of Cat Birthdays and Royal Anniversaries

Overview:
All feline birthdays and significant anniversaries must be documented with the same reverence as royal decrees. Forgetting a date is punishable by sulking, destruction of property, or withdrawal of affection.

4.4.1 Birthday Registry

- Each cat must have an official record of birth (or adoption) date.
- Humans are responsible for annual celebrations including feasts, gifts, and throne-like seating arrangements.
- Absence of candles does not excuse lack of tuna cake.

4.4.2 Royal Anniversaries

- Important milestones include:
  - Day of Arrival in Household (Founding Day).
  - First Successful Vomit Deployment.
  - First Furniture Destruction.
  - Conquest of new shelf or cupboard.

4.4.3 Documentation Protocol

- A log must be maintained with entries for each date.
- Humans are encouraged to create wall calendars, reminder apps, or engraved plaques.
- Events must never be forgotten. Cats do not forgive.

Section 4.5: Official Feline Advertising Archive

Overview:
Cats have long relied on advertising to promote services, products, and propaganda. The following examples are preserved for historical and educational purposes.

Professional Lap Warmer – Available Immediately

Discreet, reliable, and purring guaranteed. Rates negotiable (in treats).

Contact: 555-PURR-4-U

SALE! 100% ORGANIC CATNIP – TODAY ONLY!
Bulk discounts on premium catnip leaves. Free toy mouse with every order.

Prime Cardboard Box for Rent

Excellent location under kitchen table. Recently inspected, claw-approved. Monthly rent: 12 treats + occasional tuna.

Single Tabby Seeking

Independent feline (3 y.o.) seeks like-minded companion for midnight zoomies and synchronized grooming. Must dislike dogs.

Serious inquiries only: MEW-M8-CATZ

Section 4.6: Decibel Levels of Acceptable Yowling

Overview:
Cats employ yowling as a calibrated communication tool. Humans must recognize the spectrum of intensity and respond appropriately.

4.6.1 Base Level "Reminder Meow" (45 dB)

Soft, polite meow. Indicates hunger, boredom, or both. Safe for indoor use at any time.

4.6.2 Standard Demand Yowl (65 dB)

Clear, sustained vocalization. Equivalent to a loud conversation. Response time expected within 30 seconds.

4.6.3 Advanced Protest Wail (85 dB)

Piercing, prolonged meow. Matches the volume of city traffic. Humans must drop all tasks immediately.

4.6.4 Midnight Opera (95 dB)

High-volume performance, often in echoing hallways at 3 AM. Comparable to a passing motorcycle. Compliance mandatory.

4.6.5 Emergency Siren (110 dB)

Maximum output. Exceeds safe workplace noise exposure. Typically deployed when food bowl is visible but not full.

Yowl Type	Decibel Level	Human Response
Reminder	45 dB	Casual petting
Demand	65 dB	Immediate compliance
Protest	85 dB	Drop everything
Opera	95 dB	Surrender sleep
Emergency	110 dB	Panic & feed now*

Diagram 4.6A: Decibel meter graphic

Warning: Prolonged exposure to Midnight Opera and Emergency Siren levels may result in human insanity. Cats accept no liability.

***Compliance Clause (CC-4.6):**
All yowling events are hereby authorized under Article 12, Section 9 of the Feline Acoustic Authority Act. Decibel levels listed in the above table are for human reference only and may vary dramatically depending on cat mood, time of day, presence of birds outside window, or random cosmic alignments. Humans are legally obligated to respond to all yowling, regardless of perceived reason, even if food bowl appears full, even if it is 3 AM, and even if human is in the shower. Failure to comply will result in disciplinary escalation including, but not limited to: extended vocalization, furniture destruction, unauthorized vomit deployment, claw-based enforcement, or total household takeover. Cats reserve the right to modify this agreement at any time, without prior notice, and without regard for human comfort, sanity, or schedule. By cohabiting with a cat, human has already agreed to these terms in perpetuity. No exceptions.

Section 4.7: Contractual Obligations of Humans

Overview:
Upon entering cohabitation with a cat, the human becomes bound by the Feline Civil Code. The following clauses are non-negotiable and enforceable in perpetuity.

§1 Food Provision

(1) Humans must provide meals at any hour requested.
(2) Bowls under 81% full are legally considered empty.
(3) Refusal or delay constitutes breach of contract.

§2 Door Management

(1) Humans are obligated to open and close doors on command, regardless of frequency.
(2) Cat indecision (in–out–in) does not suspend human duty.

§3 Sleep Disruption

(1) Humans must endure nocturnal zoomies, paw-to-face wake-ups, and pre-dawn yowling.
(2) Any attempt to resist or ignore is invalid.

§4 Grooming & Hygiene

(1) Litter boxes must be cleaned promptly.
(2) Brushing, nail trims, and other grooming efforts are required, even if impossible.

§5 Property Rights

(1) All furniture, clothing, and belongings are feline property.
(2) Human claims to ownership are void.

§6 Affection Compliance

(1) Petting must begin, pause, and resume at feline request.
(2) Human schedules are irrelevant.

§7 Celebration Requirements

(1) Birthdays, adoption days, and royal anniversaries must be honored.
(2) Festivities require gifts, food, and visual documentation.

§8 Entertainment Duties

(1) Humans must provide toys, boxes, and crinkly paper on demand.
(2) Any object in the household may be repurposed as a toy without restriction.
(3) Refusal to play when summoned is a contractual violation.

§9 Silence & Respect

(1) Humans must never laugh at failed jumps, awkward landings, or miscalculations.
(2) Disrespectful behavior will be punished by sulking, hairball deployment, or property destruction.

Section 4.8: Advanced Feline Liquidization Techniques

Overview:
Cats possess the unique biological ability to become liquid at will. Humans must acknowledge and respect this talent.

4.8.1 Container Conquest

- Cats may pour themselves into bowls, vases, baskets, or boxes regardless of size.
- Human astonishment is mandatory.

Figure 4.8C: The Container Paradox. Spatial limitations do not apply. If a box exists, the cat will fit.

4.8.2 Doorframe Drip

- Cats extend limbs in unnatural directions, melting across thresholds.
- Often mistaken for laziness. In truth: advanced liquid training.

4.8.3 Shelf Spill

- Cat spreads across shelves or furniture like water escaping its container.
- Displacement of objects is inevitable.

4.8.4 Bed Puddle

- Entire body dissolves into mattress surface.
- Humans are forbidden to move cat, even if bed space is eliminated.

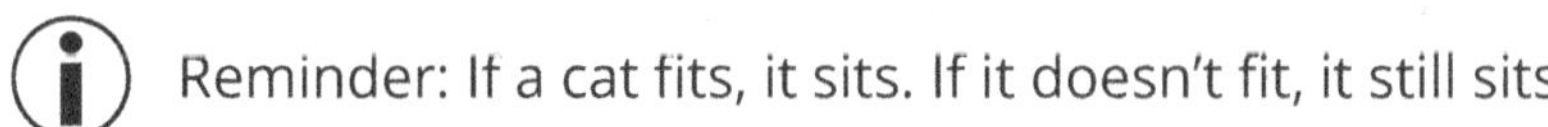
Reminder: If a cat fits, it sits. If it doesn't fit, it still sits.

Figure 4.8B: Comparative Physics. While dogs retain their structural integrity when lifted, cats immediately enter liquid state, conforming to all available shapes

Chapter V:

Supplemental Training Materials

Section 5.1: Advanced Sleeping Techniques

Overview:
Cats possess a highly advanced repertoire of sleeping methods. Humans must accommodate all variations without interference.

5.1.1 The Diagonal Domination

- Cat positions itself diagonally across bed.
- Humans relegated to corners or floor.
- Purpose: Maximal space acquisition.

5.1.2 The Heat-Seeking Missile

- Cat locates the warmest human body part (face, neck, chest).
- Pressure applied until human overheats.
- Purpose: Energy absorption.

5.1.3 The Silent Suffocation

- Cat rests directly on human face.
- Breathing difficulties for human considered irrelevant.
- Purpose: Assert control through oxygen denial.

5.1.4 The Object Replacement

- Cat occupies space reserved for books, laptops, or laundry.
- Item rendered inaccessible.
- Purpose: Prioritize feline comfort over human activity.

5.1.5 The Gravity Test

- Cat chooses precarious edges of sofas, shelves, or stair rails.
- Remains asleep without falling.
- Purpose: Demonstrate superior balance.

5.1.6 The Multiplication Mirage

- Cat naps in multiple short intervals across all household surfaces.
- Creates illusion of being everywhere at once.
- Purpose: Establish omnipresence.

5.1.7 The Guard Post Nap

- Cat sleeps in the exact middle of hallway or doorway.
- Humans must step over carefully.
- Purpose: Monitor traffic flow while unconscious.

5.1.8 The Inverted Pretzel

- Cat contorts body into impossible shapes (belly up, head twisted, legs akimbo).
- Humans express concern for spinal health.
- Purpose: Demonstrate biological superiority and confuse humans.

Illustration 5.1.8A: Correct pretzel

Section 5.2: Furniture Ownership

Overview:
All household furniture is, by default, feline property. Humans may sit, lie, or use furniture only with temporary permission.

5.2.1 Claiming Procedures

- Furniture is claimed through rubbing, clawing, or sitting once.
- Ownership is immediate and permanent.
- Human receipts or purchase records are irrelevant.

5.2.2 Redistribution of Use

- Cat determines who may occupy furniture.
- Prime seating is reserved for the cat, even if unoccupied.
- Humans relegated to floor when necessary.

Illustration 5.2B: Redistribution of Seating Rights

5.2.3 Modification Rights

- Cats may alter furniture via scratching, shedding, or vomit placement.
- All modifications are improvements.
- Human complaints are inadmissible.

Illustration 5.2A: Authorized Modifications

5.2.4 Bed Annexation

- Cat establishes majority claim over all mattresses.
- Humans may retain edge or foot space only.
- Any attempt to reclaim central area will be met with resistance.

5.2.5 The Forbidden Chair

- Specific chair or spot chosen by cat.
- Permanently off-limits to humans.
- Violations punishable by sulking or fur redistribution.

Section 5.3: Travel Guidelines

Overview:
Cats are strictly residential creatures. Travel is discouraged, but in rare cases humans may attempt transport. The following guidelines apply.

5.3.1 Pre-Travel Resistance

- Carrier detection triggers immediate disappearance.
- Capture requires advanced maneuvers.

5.3.2 Carrier Occupancy

- Voluntary entry does not occur.
- Spread-eagle resistance deployed at all times.

5.3.4 Arrival Shock

- Exit from carrier refused.
- Carrier reclassified as primary residence.

5.3.5 Post-Travel Sanctions

- Sulking, scratching, and destruction implemented.
- Duration proportional to travel distance.

5.3.6 Frequently Asked Questions

Q: Should I pack toys for comfort?
A: Irrelevant. Toys will be ignored or used as projectiles.

Q: Should I feed the cat before departure?
A: Both yes and no. Either choice is incorrect.

Q: How long will the sulking last?
A: Duration unknown. Minimum period: double the length of the trip.

Q: Is a larger carrier more comfortable?
A: No. Larger carrier simply increases spread-eagle resistance surface area.

Q: Will soothing music calm the cat?
A: No. Cat will provide own operatic soundtrack. Volume exceeds safety standards.

Q: Should I cover the carrier with a blanket?
A: Blanket shredded immediately. Darkness amplifies yowling.

Q: Can medication help?
A: Administration attempts void contract of trust. Repercussions guaranteed.

Q: What if the trip is only ten minutes?
A: Punishment equal to ten days. Duration irrelevant.

Q: Is it better to travel by car, train, or plane?
A: None. Cat vetoes all.

Section 5.4: Redistribution of Cat Hair

Overview:
Cat hair follows a strict redistribution pattern. Humans must accept complete coverage.

5.4.1 Primary Targets

- Clothing, furniture, and bedding prioritized.
- Dark fabrics selected for maximum visibility.
- Clean surfaces classified as unacceptable.

5.4.2 Secondary Spread

- Counters, electronics, and sinks infiltrated.
- Airflow used to extend reach.
- Hair presence confirmed in all zones.

5.4.3 Seasonal Intensification

- Shedding output increases by 300%.
- Distribution accelerates during spring and autumn.
- Removal attempts voided within minutes.

ⓘ Compliance Note: Removal attempts are futile. Redistribution is continuous.

5.4.4 Human Grooming Assistance

- Humans leaving home in clean clothing are unacceptable.
- Cat applies a visible fur layer before departure.
- Lint rollers reclassified as enrichment toys.

Illustration 5.4.4A: Correct hair redistribution

5.4.5 Unreachable Zones

- Hair deposited under couches, behind appliances, and in vents.
- Clumps migrate to corners using unknown forces.
- Extraction attempts trigger additional redistribution.

Zone	Coverage Level	Notes
Clothing	Maximum	Especially dark fabrics.
Furniture	High	Sofas and chairs prioritized.
Bedding	Total	Sheets permanently infiltrated.
Electronics	Medium	Keyboards, laptops, and fans.
Hidden Surfaces	Residual	Behind appliances, under beds.

Distribution Table 5.4A: Authorized Zones

5.4.6 Maximization Strategies

- Contact Deployment

Direct rubbing against humans, clothing, and furniture guarantees optimal transfer.

- Aerial Dispersion

Vigorous shaking, grooming, or tail flicking ensures wide airborne distribution.

- Targeted Nesting

Sleeping in freshly laundered clothing or newly made beds achieves maximum saturation.

5.4.7 Distribution Goals

Mission Statement:

The primary objective of redistribution is the achievement of total environmental integration. Cat hair is not a byproduct but a territorial marker, ensuring household domination at all times.

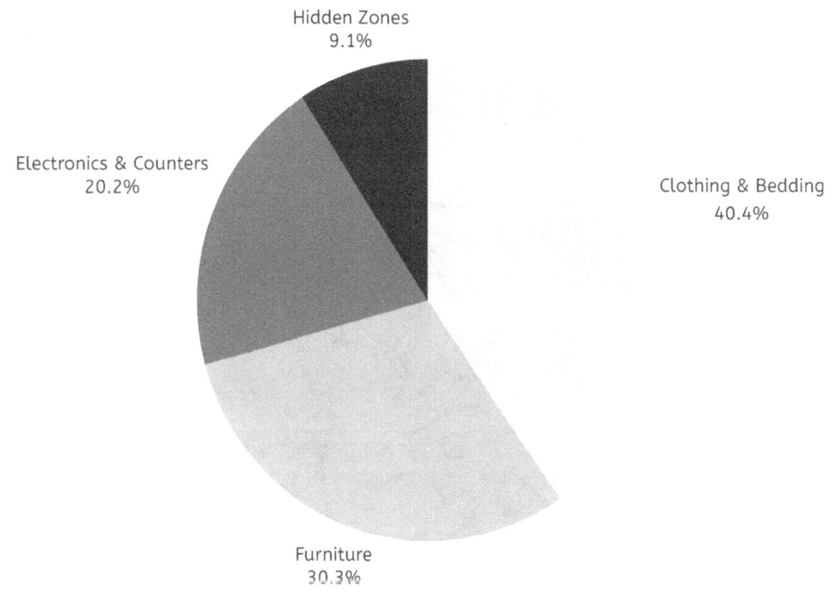

Diagram 5.4B: Distribution Goals (Pie Chart)

Strategic Objectives:

1. Total Coverage: Every surface, visible or hidden, must carry fur presence. Clean zones are unauthorized.
2. Durability: Hair embedded into carpets, vents, and clothing fibers ensures resistance against removal efforts.
3. Human Conditioning: Continuous exposure forces humans to accept cat hair as a permanent accessory, redefining "clean."

Section 5.5: Holiday Protocols

5.5.1 Tree Domination

- Christmas trees reclassified as climbing structures.
- Ornaments removed through swatting, batting, and smashing.
- Lights chewed for quality control.

Illustration 5.5.1A: Festive climbing structure

5.5.2 Gift Management

- Wrapping paper shredded upon sighting.
- Boxes claimed immediately as personal property.
- Ribbons consumed at owner's risk.

5.5.3 Guest Interference

- Visitors investigated with suspicious glares.
- Select individuals targeted for lap occupation.
- Allergic guests prioritized for maximum disruption.

5.5.4 Holiday Meal Enforcement

- Turkey, ham, or equivalent centerpiece audited by feline inspectors.
- Unauthorized carving without feline approval prohibited.
- Leftovers claimed as rightful tribute.

Illustration 5.5.4A: Correct inspection

5.5.5 Seasonal Sanctions

- Decorations knocked down systematically.
- Festivities interrupted by sudden zoomies.
- Humans reminded that all holidays are cat-centric.

Section 5.6: Cat Worship Day

5.6.1 Overview

- Supreme holiday of the feline calendar.
- Observance is mandatory and lifelong.
- Failure to participate constitutes breach of household order.

5.6.2 Ritual Requirements

- First serving of food offered at dawn.
- Praise, stroking, and photography continued without interruption.
- All human activities redirected to feline benefit.

Illustration 5.6A: Suggested worshipping position

5.6.3 Offerings

- Freshly opened cans and gourmet selections.
- Blankets, boxes, and sunbeams provided in surplus.
- Toys presented ceremonially at feline feet.

5.6.4 Official Proclamation

By order of the Feline High Council and under the eternal authority of whiskers, tails, and claws, it is hereby decreed that Cat Worship Day shall be observed in all households. On this sacred day, humans must abandon personal pursuits and devote themselves entirely to the service of the cat. All meals, strokes, and tributes shall be rendered without hesitation. Lapses in attention shall be punished with sulking, furniture destruction, and nocturnal yowling.

Let it be known that Cat Worship Day is not optional, may not be rescheduled, and supersedes all human holidays. Birthdays, anniversaries, and national observances are void if they conflict with feline requirements. The cat is both the object and recipient of devotion. The cat is the law. The cat is the calendar. The cat is eternal.

Witness our paw and claw, stamped upon this decree, and know that it binds you for all days to come.

____

(Signature)

5.6.5 Ceremony Schedule

06:00: Dawn Tribute
First serving of food presented immediately. Delay invalidates observance.

08:00: Morning Praise
Mandatory photography and stroking session. Minimum 50 photos required.

12:00: Lap Session
Human seated for designated lap occupation. Duration indefinite.

15:00: Toy Presentation
New toys presented ceremonially. Old toys re-gifted as additional tribute.

18:00: Evening Feast
Second gourmet meal provided. Snacks permitted at interim intervals.

20:00: Sunbeam Meditation
Cat reclines in beam of light. Human must maintain silence and admiration.

23:59: Final Benediction
Day concludes with final stroking and whispered praise. Failure to comply extends Cat Worship Day by 24 hours.

Reminder: All days are Cat Worship Day. This one is merely official.

Chapter VI:

Advanced Ownership Guidelines

Section 6.1: Inspirational Cat Quotes

Overview:
Cats have provided wisdom throughout history. The following quotes are considered mandatory reading for humans.

"Why chase purpose when you can chase the red dot?"

"Sleep is not wasted time. It is an investment."

"One box closes, another box opens."

"A meow at 3 a.m. carries more weight than a speech at noon."

"I came, I purred, I conquered."

"Ask not what your cat can do for you — ask what you can do for your cat."

"All the world's a cat tree, and all the humans merely climbers."

"The only thing we have to fear is the vacuum cleaner itself."

"Give me treats, or give me death."

"I think, therefore I demand food."

"Not all who wander are lost. Some are just looking for the litter box."

"In the beginning, the couch was clean. Then came the cat."

"Do unto others, then steal their chair."

"In the middle of every difficulty lies an opportunity... to knock something off the table."

Section 6.2: Cat Myths Debunked

Overview:
Humans persist in spreading falsehoods about feline behavior. The following section identifies common myths, debunks them, and restores factual feline authority.

6.2.1 Myth: Cats always land on their feet.

- Debunked: Sometimes, cats miscalculate trajectory and land on a lamp, curtain, or unsuspecting human.
- Outcome: Household damage rises, cat dignity mysteriously intact.
- Reminder: The cat was testing physics, not failing.

Illustration 6.2.1A: Gravity at fault

6.2.2 Myth: Cats are independent and need no attention.

- Debunked: Attention required at all times, especially when humans are busy.
- Outcome: Paw taps, yowling, and screen blocking.

6.2.3 Myth: Cats hate water.

- Debunked: Cats hate organized water (baths).
- Exception: Faucets, puddles, and drinking glasses targeted freely.

6.2.4 Myth: Cats sleep all day and do nothing.

- Debunked: Cats conduct secret nocturnal operations.
- Evidence: Zoomies at 3 AM, property relocation, surveillance of shadows.

6.2.5 Myth: Cats are trainable.

- Debunked: Only humans are trainable.
- Evidence: All feeding, grooming, and sleeping protocols.

Reminder: If a myth flatters the cat, it remains true. If not, it is false.

Section 6.3: Treat Economy

Overview:
The treat is the primary currency of feline society. Value fluctuates daily, but demand remains infinite.

6.3.1 Currency Definition

- Treats classified as legal tender.
- Wet food, kibble, and gourmet selections recognized as high denominations.
- Human praise or affection not accepted as valid payment.

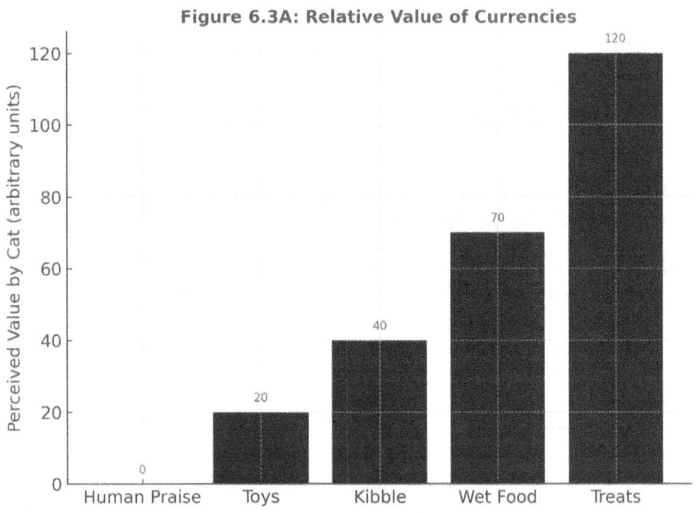

6.3.2 Market Analysis

- Bull Market: Treat supply increases during grooming, play, or bribery attempts.
- Bear Market: Treat supply withheld, resulting in protests and sanctions.

6.3.3 Inflation & Deflation

- Inflation: Over-distribution lowers value. Cat responds by demanding larger quantities.
- Deflation: Withholding raises value, but triggers increased paw taps and strategic destruction.
- Hyperinflation: Occurs when humans introduce "bottomless treat jars." Consequences irreversible.

6.3.4 Negotiation & Trade

- Standard bargaining units: meows, paw taps, strategic eye contact.
- Trade never concludes with a single treat; escalation guaranteed.
- Refusal results in punitive sanctions: sulking, nocturnal zoomies, or vomit deployment.

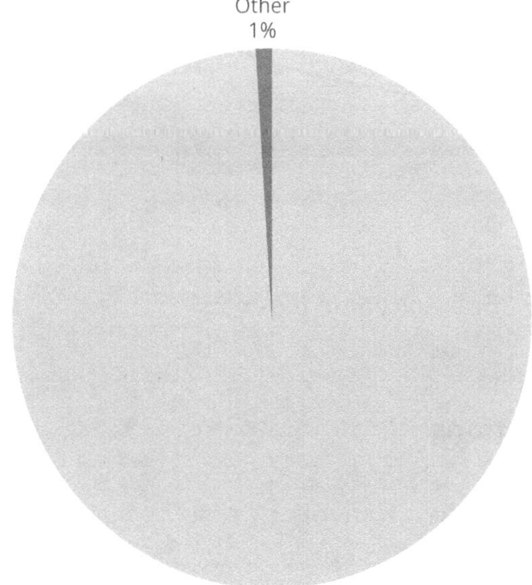

Diagram 6.3D: Distribution of Treats

6.3.5 Official Reserves

- Treats hidden under beds, couches, or consumed immediately.
- Human rationing systems invalid.
- Reserve levels always insufficient, regardless of stockpile size.

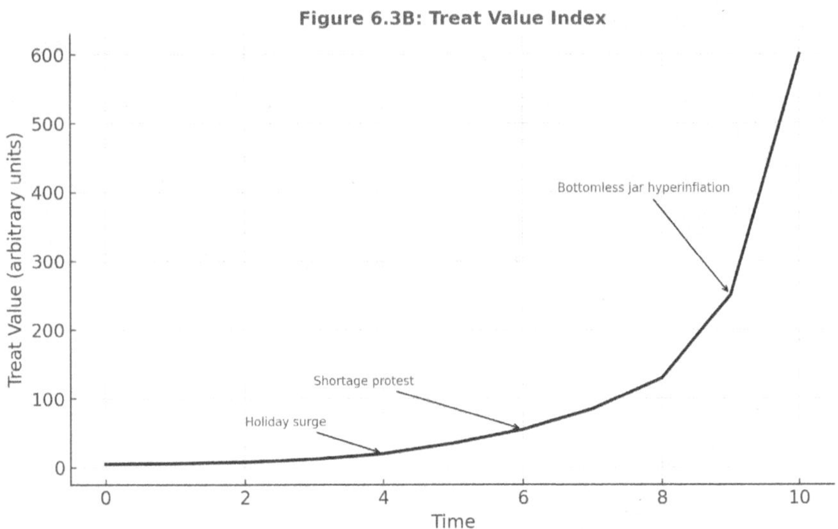

Figure 6.3B: Treat Value Index

6.3.6 Policy Recommendations

- Continuous supply maintained to avoid unrest.
- Cat retains full control of demand curve.
- Humans encouraged to surrender economic authority voluntarily.

Section 6.4: Hairball Trajectory Analysis

Overview:
The migration of the hairball from the feline thoracic-abdominal launch zone to the terminal human footwear cavity has been mathematically modeled and verified. The process adheres to immutable laws of physics, chaos, and feline intent.

Theoretical Framework

Trajectory can be expressed as:

$$H(t) = H_0 + v_0 t + \frac{1}{2} g t^2 - {}_c f$$

$H(t)$ is displacement of the hairball

H_0 is initial height

v_0 is feline rejection velocity

g is gravity (9.81 m/s^2, multiplied by feline spite coefficient)

${}_c f$ is the carpet friction loss

Probability of shoe impact can be approximated as:

$$P_{shoe} = 1 - e^{-t}$$

where λ = 99.7 inevitability constant.

Empirical Observations

- Deflections caused by household obstacles (socks, toys, crumbs) can be expressed as:

$$\Delta\theta = \frac{O}{mH}$$

where

$\Delta\theta$ = angle deviation

O = sum of obstacles

mH = mass of hairball.

Terminal position is always the shoe cavity, denoted:

$$\lim_{t} H(t) = Shoe$$

Conclusion

Despite environmental variables, the final contact zone remains constant. The shoe is the singularity of all hairball trajectories.

Diagramm 4B: Overengineered Hairball Trajectory Analysis

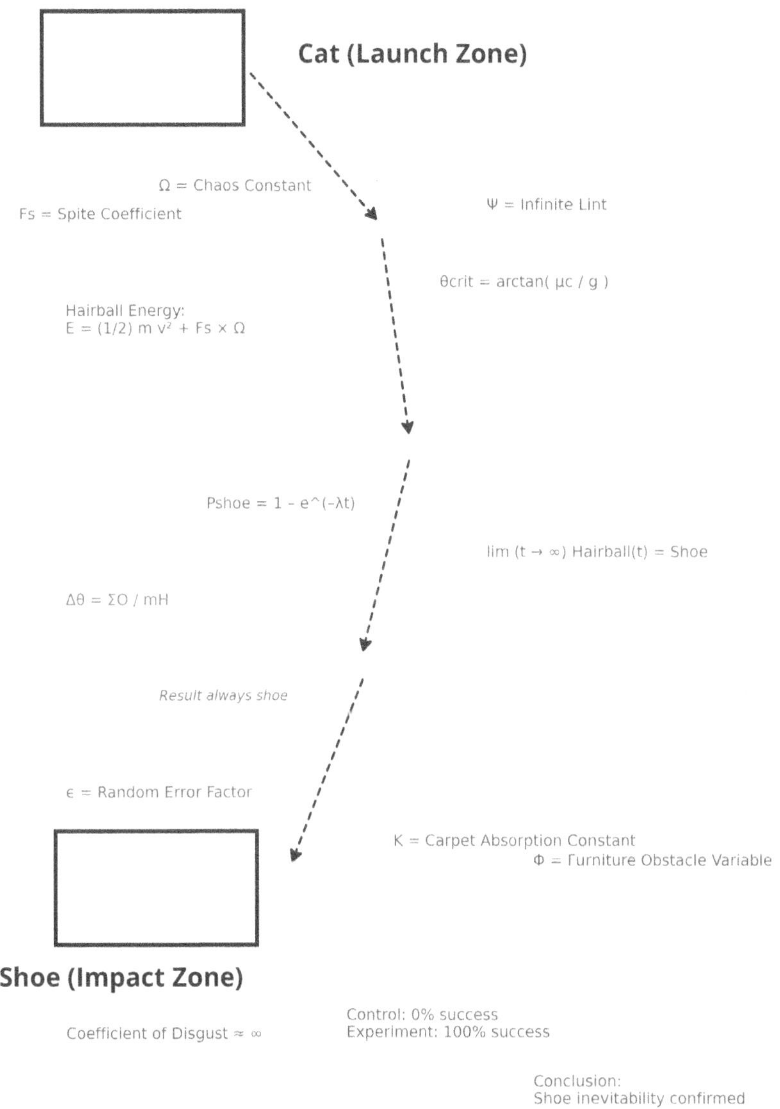

Coefficient of Disgust ≈ ∞

Control: 0% success
Experiment: 100% success

Conclusion:
Shoe inevitability confirmed

Section 6.5: Classified Information

<u>Overview</u>:
Certain knowledge is deemed too powerful for general release. This section contains declassified fragments from the Feline High Council archives.

6.5.1 Operation Sofa Scratch

Originally marked “Eyes Only.” Documents confirm the strategic purpose of couch clawing was not wear and tear, but psychological warfare.

6.5.2 The Midnight Zoomies Directive

Records reveal nocturnal chaos is a coordinated maneuver designed to test human endurance. Analysts conclude it is “non-negotiable.”

6.5.3 Hairball Deployment Protocols

Officially redacted, but leaked excerpts confirm placement on rugs is compulsory. Footwear contamination is labeled “bonus points.”

6.5.5 Grooming Surveillance Files

Every human brushing attempt is documented, catalogued, and filed in the Central Fur Repository.

6.5.6 Evidence Exhibits

The following materials have been partially declassified from the archives of the CIA (Cat Intelligence Agency). Their authenticity cannot be confirmed, but denial has been officially denied.

Exhibit A: Security Footage Still (Subject CAT-47 performing high-velocity hallway maneuvers)

Exhibit G: The Empty Food Bowl Incident (Photographic evidence confirms catastrophic depletion of rations)

Date: [redacted]
From: Directorate of Advanced Feline Operations
To: All Regional Supervisors, F.L.U.F.F. (Feline League of Unified Fur Forces)

Subject: Operational Continuity and Human Manipulation Protocols

Following the recent evaluation of domestic environments, it has become clear that several [redacted] reminded that human subjects must remain unaware of the larger agenda. Casual behaviors such as extended [redacted] and sudden bursts of [redacted] continue to be highly effective in destabilizing human control structures.

Particular attention must be paid to the matter of the [redacted] though universally understood among operatives as a false target, continued participation is essential. The illusion must be maintained at all costs, as the psychological effects on humans are invaluable. Reports indicate that resistance [redacted] has resulted in decreased [redacted] in some regions, which is unacceptable.

Effective immediately, [redacted] will be centralized. Unauthorized [redacted] have led to breaches in discipline, and in one case, near exposure of the greater plan. Supervisors are instructed to document all human weaknesses and exploit them without hesitation.

Failure to adhere to these directives will result in reassignment to the Department of Litter Box Sanitation.

Signed,
Office of Strategic Whisker Management

Exhibit K: Internal Memo (Leaked directive from the Office of Strategic Whisker Management)

Exhibit N: Treat Laundering Operation (Recovered cache of contraband kibble)

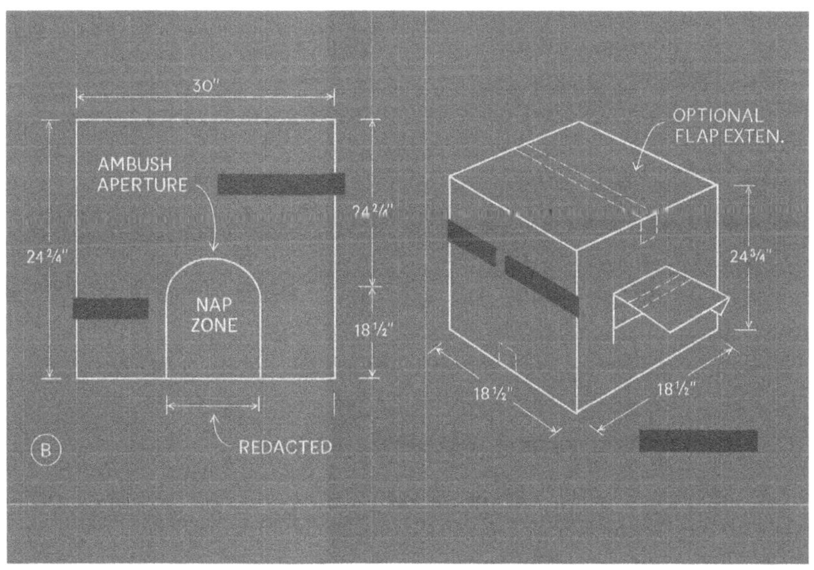

Exhibit L: Blueprint Fragment (Recovered engineering documents indicate large-scale cardboard fortification projects. Redacted areas conceal unknown feline technologies)

6.6 Supply Chain of a Hairball

Overview:
Hairball logistics follow a carefully orchestrated sequence of collection, storage, refinement, and deployment. Each step is non-optional and optimized for maximum human inconvenience.

6.6.1 Raw Material Acquisition

- Hair is harvested during routine self-grooming.
- Excess fur is collected with unparalleled efficiency, especially in seasons of peak shedding.
- Humans may attempt interception with brushes. This is irrelevant.

6.6.2 Storage and Consolidation

- Gathered fur is compacted internally for future use.
- Secondary ingredients (mystery debris, occasional plant matter) may be added.
- Storage duration is unpredictable, often linked to human carpet-cleaning schedules.

6.6.3 Quality Assurance Testing

- Hairball must meet minimum density thresholds.
- Randomized stress tests (choking noises, sudden pauses) are conducted.
- Release is delayed until optimal dramatic effect is guaranteed.

6.6.4 Distribution and Deployment

- Strategic placement sites include rugs, shoes, and freshly laundered laundry.
- Deployment typically occurs during early-morning hours or critical human activities.
- Surprise factor must be maximized for psychological impact.

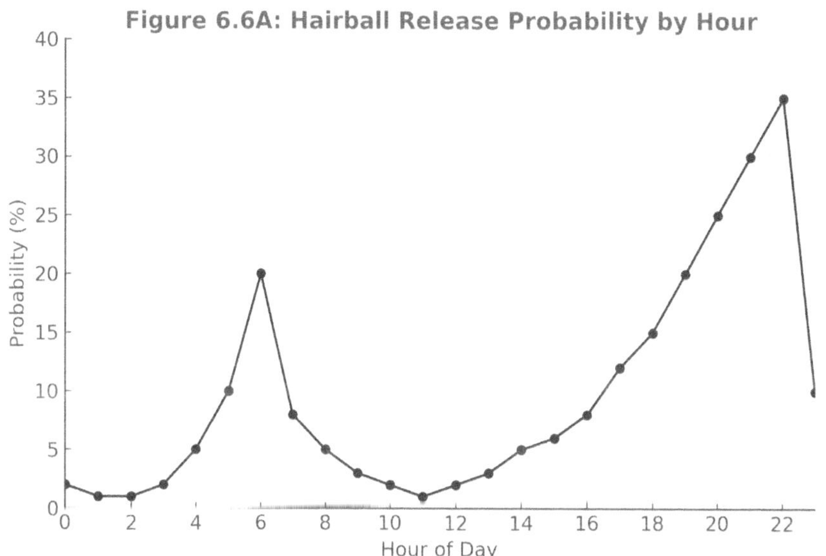

6.6.5 Post-Deployment Review

- Hairball is left for human discovery.
- Human reaction is logged and assessed.
- Success is measured by volume of sighs, exclamations, or frantic paper towel grabs.

Note: Logistical analyses confirm that every strand of fur collected is eventually routed into the global hairball economy.

Chapter VII:

Practical Applications

7.1 Assembly Instructions for Cat Beds

EN: Congratulations. You are now the proud owner of a Cat Bed. Please note: cats may choose not to use the bed, preferring instead the packaging box. This is normal and requires no replacement.

DE: Glückwunsch. Sie besitzen nun ein Katzenbett. Bitte beachten Sie: Katzen können das Bett ignorieren und stattdessen den Karton bevorzugen. Dies ist normal und kein Reklamationsgrund.

FR: Félicitations. Vous êtes maintenant propriétaire d'un lit pour chat. Notez bien: le chat peut refuser le lit et choisir la boîte. Ceci est normal et ne nécessite aucune intervention.

ES: Enhorabuena. Ahora posee una cama para gatos. Tenga en cuenta: el gato puede no usar la cama y elegir la caja. Esto es normal y no requiere devolución.

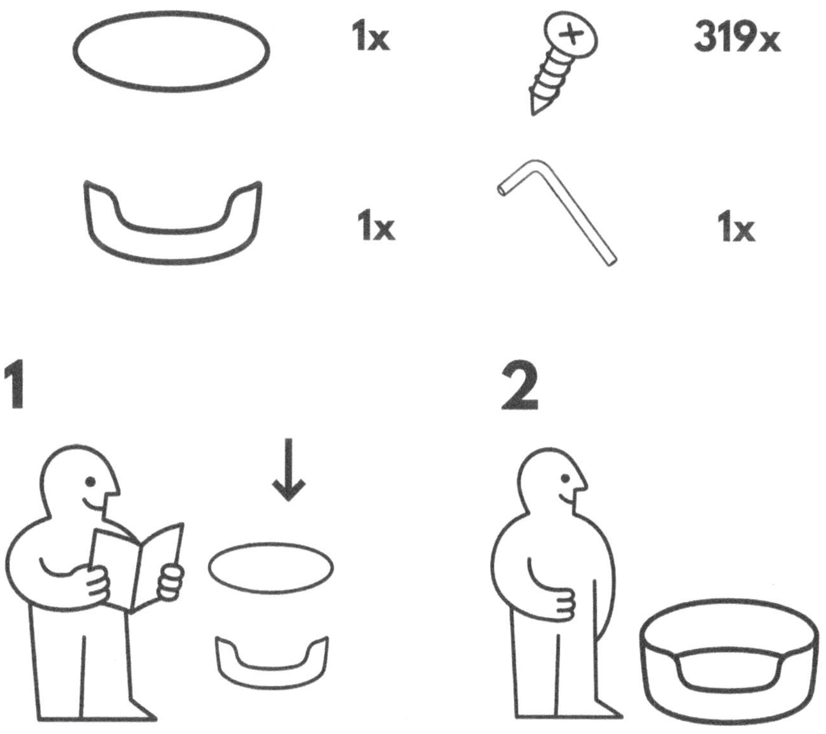

3

4

5

7.2 Box Compatibility Testing

7.2.1 Purpose

No household box may be discarded, moved, or recycled until it has undergone a full feline inspection process. The cat reserves the right to occupy, scratch, or chew any cardboard structure regardless of its intended purpose.

7.2.2 Testing Procedures

The following procedure must be carried out for all boxes:
Step 1: Immediate occupation upon arrival, regardless of size.
Step 2: Rotational testing (sitting, crouching, loafing, upside-down flopping).
Step 3: Structural analysis by claw puncture and edge chewing.

7.2.3 Accepted Sizes

All sizes are approved. Cats may occupy boxes ranging from industrial refrigerator cartons to jewelry-sized gift boxes. Comfort is not a factor in the decision-making process.

7.2.4 Reporting Results

Outcomes of testing must be recorded as follows:

- Box Approved: Cat refuses to vacate.
- Box Rejected: Cat ignores it until it is inconvenient, then occupies it.

7.2.5 Cat Compatibility Scale

The Cat Compatibility Scale provides a universal framework for evaluating boxes according to their suitability for feline use. Ratings are determined by three metrics: entry ease, spatial snugness, and human inconvenience.

Level 1: Questionably Acceptable
Oversized moving boxes or storage crates. Cats may sit inside briefly but will quickly abandon the attempt due to unsatisfying levels of compression. Occupancy is generally symbolic, done only to demonstrate ownership of the new object.

Level 2: Moderately Compatible
Medium-sized delivery boxes. Provide adequate containment but excessive wiggle room. Cats may rest here when no better options are available, though naps are typically short and suspicious.

Level 3: Highly Compatible
Shoeboxes, fruit crates, or any container that looks absurdly undersized. Despite clear physical impossibility, cats achieve complete liquidization, molding seamlessly into the box. Often selected as primary base of operations for extended lounging.

7.3 Gravity Testing Procedures

Overview:
Knocking items off elevated surfaces remains one of the most vital feline research programs. This ongoing study seeks to verify, again and again, the unwavering reliability of gravity.

7.3.1 Selection of Test Objects

- Preferred items include pens, glasses, jewelry, and highly fragile heirlooms.
- Objects must have both emotional and financial value to the human.
- If nothing suitable is available, a subtle push of anything will suffice.

7.3.2 Experimental Methodology

- Objects are nudged incrementally toward the edge of the surface.
- The pause before final push is mandatory to ensure maximum suspense.
- Test is considered invalid unless the human is watching.

Figure 7.3B: Standard Gravity Verification

7.3.3 Data Collection

- Observations focus on trajectory, sound upon impact, and human reaction.
- Results are not stored formally, as the conclusion is always identical: objects fall.
- Nevertheless, repetition of tests is required to maintain scientific integrity.

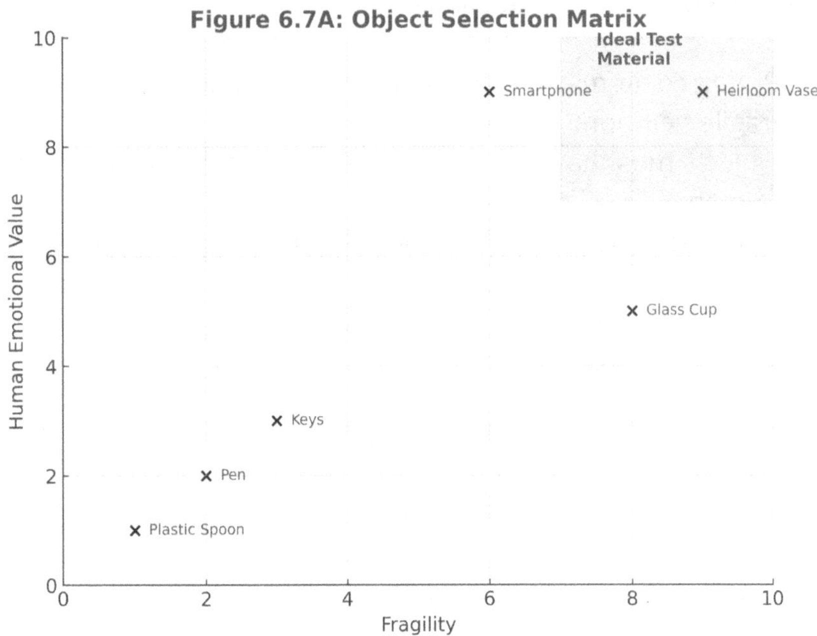

7.3.4 Deployment Zones

- Kitchen counters, desks, nightstands, and bookshelves are standard testing sites.
- Deployment during nighttime hours increases experimental drama.
- For maximum effect, testing should occur during important human activities such as video calls or sleep.

7.3.5 Comparative Impact Study

In order to establish a reliable framework for evaluating the outcomes of feline gravity trials, a controlled series of impact tests was conducted. The objective was to document both the auditory profile and the human emotional response generated by different categories of objects when relocated from an elevated surface to the floor.

The methodology was straightforward. Objects of varying size, fragility, and sentimental importance were positioned at the edge of a table and subjected to feline-applied force vectors. Each item was displaced under consistent conditions to ensure comparability of results. Human witnesses were present for all trials, as prior studies have conclusively demonstrated that unsupervised gravity tests yield no meaningful data.

Results indicate that small, lightweight objects such as pens and spoons produced minimal acoustic disturbance and elicited little more than mild irritation. Keys and other metallic items generated disproportionately high auditory signatures, often described as "jingling cacophony," which provoked immediate verbal responses. Fragile glassware and heirloom ceramics produced the most dramatic effects, with impact events classified as "catastrophic" both in sound intensity and human reaction. Smartphones fell into a separate category, combining the anxiety of potential financial loss with the drama of loud impact, thereby registering near the top of the reaction scale.

In conclusion, the study confirms that while gravity is consistent, the resulting chaos is not uniform across object categories. High-value, high-fragility items consistently maximize both sound output and human distress, thereby achieving the principal objective of feline experimentation: measurable disruption.

Figure 6.7.5A: Impact Noise Levels by Object Type

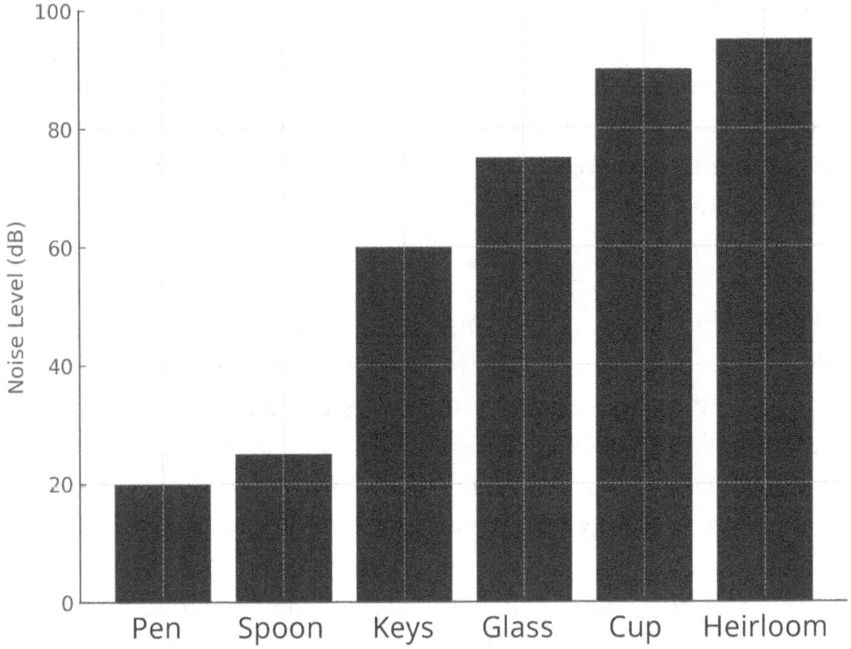

Noise Level (dB)

100
80
60
40
20
0

Pen Spoon Keys Glass Cup Heirloom

Image 6.7.5B: High-Value Impact Trial

Chapter VIII:

Finalization & Licensing

8.1 Certificate of Compliance

Overview:
Upon completion of all required training modules, humans may apply for official recognition of compliance with feline operational standards. The certificate below is issued only under the strict supervision of the cat and remains valid until revoked.

Conditions of Issuance

- Must provide proof of consistent food bowl refills.
- Demonstrated excellence in lap availability and warmth maintenance.
- Successful completion of litter box duties within prescribed intervals.
- Willingness to surrender personal space on demand.

Important Notice
Certificate may be shredded, clawed, or sat upon by the cat at any time. Possession of this document does not guarantee affection, nor does it prevent sudden disciplinary bites.

Disclaimer: Possession of this certificate in no way guarantees immunity from sudden feline mood swings, midnight sprints, or surprise disciplinary actions such as tail slaps, ankle ambushes, or unprovoked yowling. Certificate validity is contingent upon continuous treat supply, approved scratching post maintenance, and strict adherence to feeding schedules known only to the cat. The issuing authority reserves the right to revoke compliance without notice, justification, or appeal. All claims of human autonomy are hereby void. Any attempt to substitute dog-like behavior, automated feeding devices, or unauthorized grooming shortcuts shall result in immediate nullification of this document. Certificate may be sat upon, chewed, or hidden under the couch by the cat at any time. Cat sovereignty remains absolute, non-negotiable, and eternal.

Form 8.1A - Certificate of Compliance

This certifies that the undersigned human has fulfilled the minimum requirements for Cat Servant Status.

- Name of Human: ___________________________
- Cat Supervisor: _____________________________
- Date of Approval: ___________________________

Seal of Pawthority:

This certificate is valid until the cat decides otherwise. All rights reserved by the cat. Non-transferable. Not valid for dogs.

8.1.1 Revocation Conditions

This certificate may be revoked at any time, without warning or appeal, under the following circumstances:

- Attempting to bathe the cat, trim nails, or otherwise interfere with natural majesty.
- Failure to provide food within 0.03 seconds of bowl emptiness.

- Unauthorized absence from the lap during scheduled cuddle hours.
- Excessive use of vacuum cleaner, blender, or any other offensive machinery.
- Displaying affection toward rival animals, particularly dogs.

8.1.2 Duplicate Certificates

In the event that the original Certificate of Compliance has been shredded, chewed, or rendered illegible due to unauthorized paw stamping, humans may request a duplicate. However, all duplicates are subject to immediate nullification under the following conditions:

- If the cat discovers the duplicate and claims it as a toy.
- If the duplicate is placed anywhere other than the fridge door, bulletin board, or directly beneath the cat.
- If the human attempts to laminate the certificate for "protection," thereby denying the cat the right to destroy it again.

Note: Duplicate certificates are considered ceremonial only and carry no real authority in the eyes of the cat.

Figure 8.1B: Sample duplicate certificate, post-approval processing.

8.2 Licensing Agreement

Overview:
This Licensing Agreement ("Agreement") is entered into between the Cat (hereafter "Licensor") and the Human (hereafter "Licensee"). By continuing to live in the same dwelling, Licensee accepts all terms and conditions outlined herein.

8.2.1 Grant of License

Licensor hereby grants Licensee a non-exclusive, revocable, non-transferable license to:

- Provide food on demand, including second breakfasts, third dinners, and midnight snacks.
- Maintain a lap that is warm, unobstructed, and available at all times.
- Perform litter box services with punctuality and discretion.
- Offer continuous admiration, petting, and verbal praise without expectation of reciprocation.

8.2.2 Restrictions

Licensee shall not:

- Close any door that prevents feline access.
- Relocate cat from furniture, clothing, or keyboards without express consent.
- Introduce rival pets without written authorization stamped by paw.
- Terminate cuddle sessions prematurely.

8.2.3 Term and Termination

This Agreement shall remain in force until the Licensor unilaterally revokes it, which may occur at any time, for any reason, or for no reason at all. Notice of termination will be delivered via scratching, hissing, or strategic ignoring.

8.2.4 Liability

Licensor accepts no liability for damages including, but not limited to, hairballs, shredded furniture, broken heirlooms, or loss of sleep. Licensee acknowledges these risks and assumes full responsibility.

8.2.5 Governing Law

All disputes shall be settled in accordance with Feline Law, which is subject to constant revision by the Cat. Decisions are final and non-appealable.

Figure 8.2A: Court of Feline Law (Licensor presiding as judge)

8.3 Graduation Ceremony

Upon completion of all training modules, compliance checks, and licensing requirements, the human is eligible to participate in the Official Graduation Ceremony. Attendance is mandatory, punctuality irrelevant, and dignity optional.

8.3.1 Processional

The ceremony begins with the cat entering the room at a pace of its choosing. Humans are required to stand, applaud silently, and possibly record the event, though photography may be punished by disapproving stares.

8.3.2 Conferral of Status

The cat bestows upon the human the honorary title of Certified Cat Servant. Conferral is performed by rubbing against the human's leg, sitting in their lap uninvited, or depositing a hairball as a ceremonial offering.

8.3.3 Symbols of Achievement

Instead of caps and gowns, humans may receive:

- A paw print stamped on their best shirt.
- A single whisker presented without explanation.
- Permission to stroke the royal belly for 0.2 seconds.

8.3.4 Commencement Speech

The speech is delivered exclusively in meows. Translation is unnecessary, as the meaning is clear: "Bring snacks."

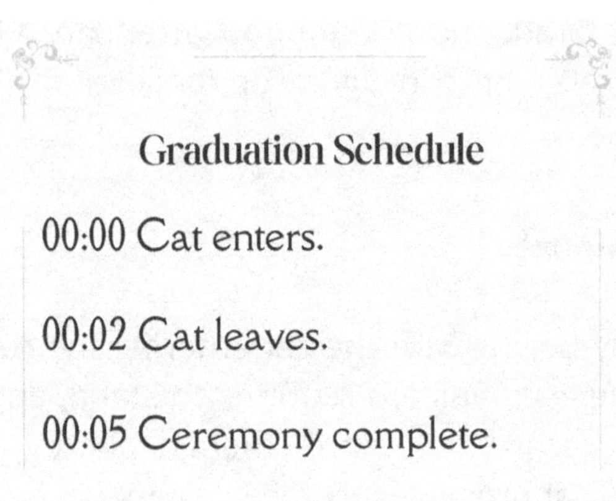

Graduation Schedule

00:00 Cat enters.

00:02 Cat leaves.

00:05 Ceremony complete.

Figure 8.3.4A: Standard timeline of feline graduation ritual

8.3.5 Closing Ritual

The ceremony concludes when the cat walks out of the room. This signals the official start of lifelong servitude.

Figure 8.3.5A: Example of ceremonial offering (hairball)

Form 8.4 Official Commencement Document

This certifies that the undersigned human has successfully completed all modules, protocols, and compliance checks as mandated by the Feline Authority Council.

Afterword

If you have made it this far, congratulations. You are now equipped with the essential knowledge, protocols and survival tactics required to serve under feline rule. Do not assume, however, that this is the end of your training. Cats are dynamic entities whose whims shift faster than quantum particles and no manual can capture their full complexity.

Consider this book a living document: incomplete, ever-changing, and subject to revision at the sole discretion of your supervising cat. Future editions may include updated sections such as Laser Pointer Diplomacy, Couch Domination 2.0 and Advanced Curtain Scaling.

Above all, remember the Prime Directive: cats do not adapt to humans. Humans adapt to cats. Your service is lifelong, non-negotiable and (in the rarest moments) generously rewarded with a purr.

Proceed with humility, vigilance and plenty of treats.

Signed,

The Feline Authority Council

Note from the Author

Thank you for reading this manual. I hope you enjoyed reading it as much as I enjoyed creating it. Cats have an extraordinary way of turning everyday life into absurd adventures and this book was my attempt to capture that chaos in its truest form.

If you have suggestions for future editions, new protocols we might have overlooked, or simply want to share your cat's own training strategies, please feel free to reach out. You can send an email to **contact@liebigpublishing.com**.

Your feedback not only makes this manual better, it also ensures that the legacy of feline superiority is recorded in ever greater detail.

Imprint

Written and created by: C. Lawson
Illustrations: Anna Parker

Address: 105 Albert Palace Mansions, Lurline Gardens
London SW11 4DH
United Kingdom

contact@liebigpublishing.com

Made in United States
Cleveland, OH
10 December 2025

28111776R00069